ATLANTA

by Diane Bailey

arcadia®
CHILDREN'S BOOKS

Published by Arcadia Children's Books
A Division of Arcadia Publishing
Charleston, SC
www.arcadiapublishing.com

Copyright © 2022 by Arcadia Children's Books
All rights reserved

Super Cities is a trademark of Arcadia Publishing, Inc.

First published 2022

Manufactured in the United States.

ISBN 978-1-4671-9893-6

Library of Congress Control Number: 2022937949

Notice: The information in this book is true and complete to the best of our knowledge. It is offered without guarantee on the part of the author or Arcadia Publishing. The author and Arcadia Publishing disclaim all liability in connection with the use of this book.

All rights reserved. No part of this book may be reproduced or transmitted in any form whatsoever without prior written permission from the publisher except in the case of brief quotations embodied in critical articles and reviews.

Produced by Shoreline Publishing Group LLC
Santa Barbara, California
Designer: Patty Kelley

Contents

Welcome to Atlanta! 4	Performing Arts 52
Map It! 6	How to Talk Atlanta 54
Made in the Shade 8	Atlanta: It's Weird 56
Atlanta Means 10	Hey! I'm From Atlanta, Too! 58
Atlanta BeltLine 12	What People Do in Atlanta 60
History: First People 14	Hollywood of the South 62
History: Building a Town 16	Eat the Atlanta Way 64
History: Out of the Ashes 18	Go, Atlanta Sports! 66
History Atlanta Grows Up 20	College Town 72
History: Civil Rights in Atlanta 22	Atlanta's HBCUs 74
History: New Directions 24	It's Alive: Animals in Atlanta 76
People from the Past 26	We Saw It at the Zoo! 78
The Home of Dr. King 28	We Saw It at the Aquarium! 80
Atlanta Neighborhoods 30	Parks 82
Why Is It So Hot and Sticky 32	Spooky Sights 84
Things to See 34	Not Far Away 86
Stone Mountain 40	Sister Cities 90
Getting Around Atlanta 44	Find Out More 92
Art in Atlanta 46	Index 94
Atlanta Museums 48	

WELCOME TO Atlanta!

In the United States, the South is a place all its own. It doesn't have an official capital city, but if it did, it would probably be Atlanta. Look at a map and you'll find Atlanta in the northern part of Georgia.

Atlanta has been the center of the South from before the Civil War in the 1860s until today. But it's not a city that's stuck in the past. It's got

FAST FACTS
Atlanta, Georgia
POPULATION:
About 500,000 just in Atlanta, 6.1 million in the greater Atlanta area
FOUNDED:
1837
NICKNAMES:
Hollywood of the South, City of Trees

a lot going on right now—from world-class museums to offbeat restaurants. And move over, Hollywood! If you've got an eagle eye, you might spot a celebrity, since the state of Georgia is becoming a favorite place to make movies.

New buildings are always going up, but next to all those shiny high-rises are nature's high-rises: trees. Atlanta is sometimes called the "city in the forest." About half of the city is covered in trees. Ready to soak up some sun and have some fun? Grab a glass of lemonade, and let's go to Atlanta!

ATLANTA: Map It!

Atlanta was founded so that the region could have a railroad line. The city is in a great location. It's pretty close to the east coast and Florida, and opens up to the Midwest to the north. Atlanta is on the way to everywhere!

Atlanta might be "down South," but it's "up" in terms of elevation. It's located in the foothills of the Appalachian Mountains, so the city is pretty high—more than 1,000 feet above sea level. It's the highest major city east of the Mississippi River.

Water flows to the sea, but which one? There's an imaginary geographical line running north to south down the middle of Atlanta called the Eastern Continental Divide. Water that falls on the south and east sides of this line ends up in the Atlantic Ocean. Rain on the north and west sides drains into the Gulf of Mexico.

A 350-foot mural called "Native Waters" recognizes the Eastern Continental Divide, and other natural features in Georgia.

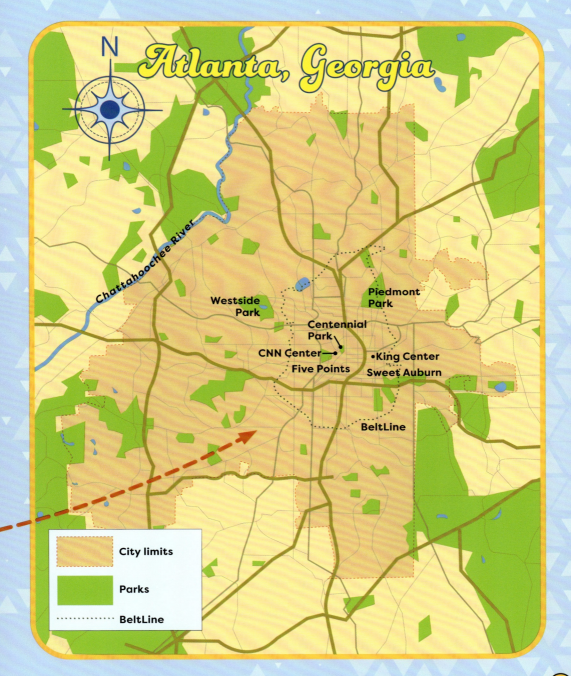

Made in the Shade

Atlanta is a good place to be a squirrel or a bird. Magnolias, hickories, giant red oaks, and other trees give the city a definite green vibe. It's one of the "tree-iest" cities in the country.

Recent years have been tough on the trees, though. Some were cut down to make room for new buildings. Plus, climate change has caused droughts in some years, and too much rainfall in others. That weakens the roots, and strong winds can topple even the tallest and strongest of trees. Fortunately, the city and volunteer groups are working to replant some of the downed trees, as well as protect historic landmark trees that have been standing for decades.

Trees Atlanta is a nonprofit organization that started in 1985 to make the city greener. The group planted 46 trees in 1986—and now they're up to more than 150,000. They have a goal of planting a million trees by 2030.

FAST FACT

Dig In: The Youth Tree Team lets high school and college students spend several weeks in the summer planting and taking care of trees on the Atlanta BeltLine.

ATLANTA MEANS...

When Atlanta began, it was actually the end. Confused? Here's the deal: back in 1837, folks wanted to build railroads to connect the eastern part of the country to the Midwest. One of the railroad lines was planned to stop in vacant land in northern Georgia. Engineers hammered in a stone railroad stake and labeled it "Mile Zero," to indicate the end of the line. The city that was built there was originally called Terminus, which means "end." A nearby settlement called Thrasherville arose to the south, when John Thrasher's company was hired to build railroad tracks. But that name didn't stick once the railroad arrived.

By 1843, the name "Terminus" name was changed to "Marthasville," because the governor at the time, Wilson Lumpkin, had a daughter named Martha. People didn't love the name, though. And Martha didn't even live there!

So, back to the railroad. The plan was to eventually build railroad lines all the way between the Atlantic and Pacific Oceans, so one suggestion was to call the city Atlantica-Pacifica. That was even more of a mouthful than Marthasville! But good news: Martha's middle name was Atalanta, so the city chose the shortened "Atlanta" for its new name.

The original zero milepost is still standing—just not at its original location. A replica (a copy) was installed there in 2018. Visitors can see the real stone post at the Atlanta History Center.

Wilson Lumpkin

This is the original "zero" milepost that showed where Atlanta began.

Atlanta

Atanta BeltLine

Hey, I've Got an Idea: Ryan Gravel was studying architecture and city planning at Georgia Tech when he proposed the idea for the BeltLine in 1999. The idea was a hit an over time has become a 33-mile series of connected trails, walkways, bike lanes, and greenspace, perfect for walking, biking, and more.

Many of Atlanta's historic neighborhoods are on the BeltLine, including Old Fourth Ward, Inman Park, Virginia-Highland, and the West End.

In an annual parade, people walk the BeltLine carrying lanterns to light up the night.

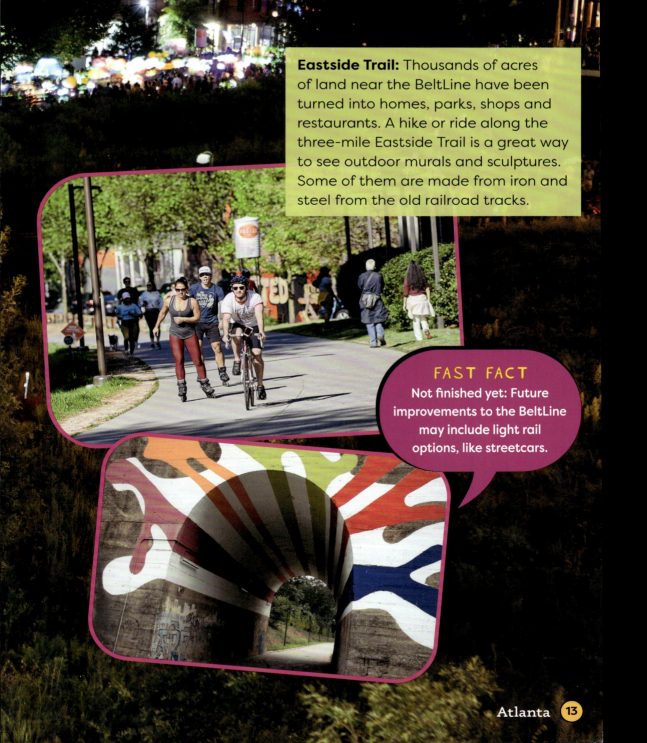

Eastside Trail: Thousands of acres of land near the BeltLine have been turned into homes, parks, shops and restaurants. A hike or ride along the three-mile Eastside Trail is a great way to see outdoor murals and sculptures. Some of them are made from iron and steel from the old railroad tracks.

FAST FACT
Not finished yet: Future improvements to the BeltLine may include light rail options, like streetcars.

History: First People

Georgia's first inhabitants lived during the Paleo-Indian period more than 10,000 years ago. These people were nomadic, meaning they traveled around most of the time. They probably hunted animals such as Columbian mammoths and giant bison, which are now extinct.

The Woodland people came after the Paleo-Indians, beginning about 3,000 years ago. They developed societies that stayed in place, using agriculture to support larger communities. Maize was one important crop.

The bow and arrow was invented during the Woodland period.

Beginning about a thousand years ago, people in the Mississippian culture built large, flat-topped earth mounds in the area around Atlanta. Important people in the community lived on top of the mounds, and ceremonies were held there.

The Cherokee and Muscogee (Creek) people were descended from the Mississippians. The Creek lived south and east of the Chattahoochee River. The Cherokee lived on the north side.

At Track Rock Gap, about two hours north of Atlanta, ancient peoples made petroglyphs, or carvings, of animals, birds, and geometric shapes. Some are still there today. A little closer to Atlanta are similar sites called Rock Hawk and Rock Eagle.

History: Building a Town

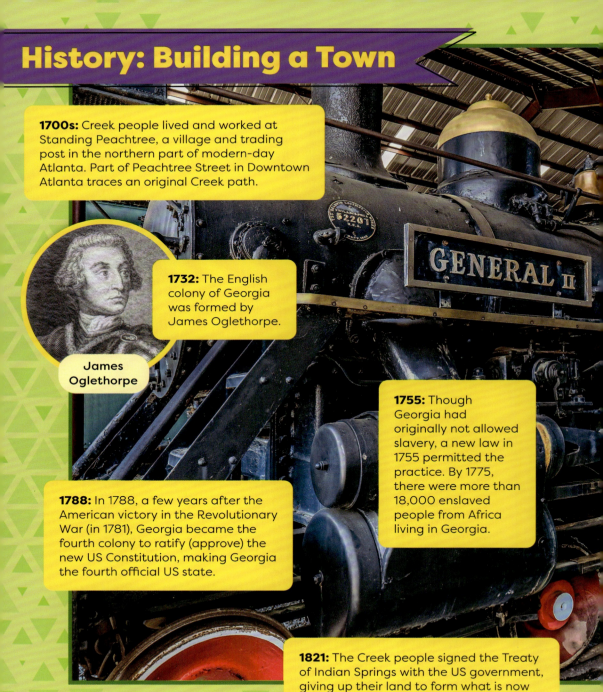

1700s: Creek people lived and worked at Standing Peachtree, a village and trading post in the northern part of modern-day Atlanta. Part of Peachtree Street in Downtown Atlanta traces an original Creek path.

1732: The English colony of Georgia was formed by James Oglethorpe.

James Oglethorpe

1755: Though Georgia had originally not allowed slavery, a new law in 1755 permitted the practice. By 1775, there were more than 18,000 enslaved people from Africa living in Georgia.

1788: In 1788, a few years after the American victory in the Revolutionary War (in 1781), Georgia became the fourth colony to ratify (approve) the new US Constitution, making Georgia the fourth official US state.

1821: The Creek people signed the Treaty of Indian Springs with the US government, giving up their land to form what is now central Atlanta and many nearby suburbs.

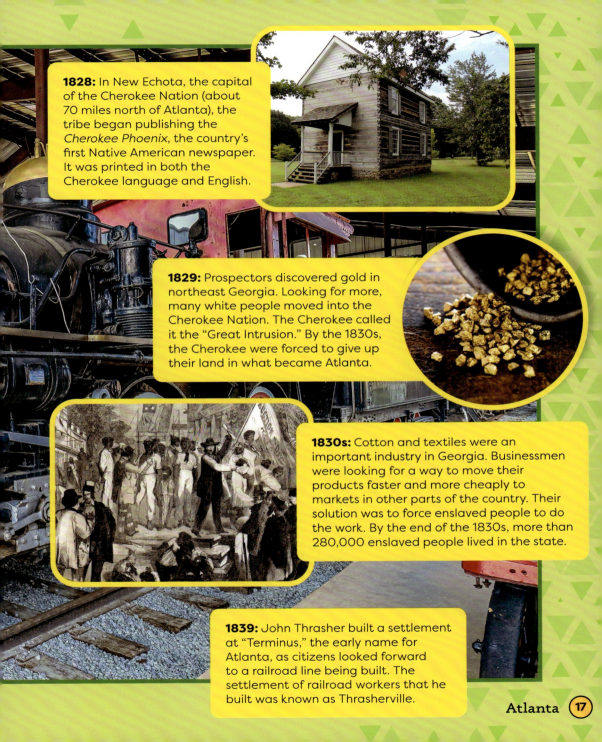

1828: In New Echota, the capital of the Cherokee Nation (about 70 miles north of Atlanta), the tribe began publishing the *Cherokee Phoenix*, the country's first Native American newspaper. It was printed in both the Cherokee language and English.

1829: Prospectors discovered gold in northeast Georgia. Looking for more, many white people moved into the Cherokee Nation. The Cherokee called it the "Great Intrusion." By the 1830s, the Cherokee were forced to give up their land in what became Atlanta.

1830s: Cotton and textiles were an important industry in Georgia. Businessmen were looking for a way to move their products faster and more cheaply to markets in other parts of the country. Their solution was to force enslaved people to do the work. By the end of the 1830s, more than 280,000 enslaved people lived in the state.

1839: John Thrasher built a settlement at "Terminus," the early name for Atlanta, as citizens looked forward to a railroad line being built. The settlement of railroad workers that he built was known as Thrasherville.

Atlanta 17

History: Out of the Ashes

1861-1865: The Civil War was fought. Georgia sided with the Confederacy, leaving the Union in an effort to keep slavery legal in Southern states. In 1864, Union armies, led by General William Tecumseh Sherman, burned the city of Atlanta, destroying more than 3,000 buildings. This event helped the North win the Civil War in 1865.

General Sherman

1865: Atlanta University (now Clark Atlanta), the city's first college for Black students, was founded to educate formerly enslaved people.

1868: Atlanta was named as the Georgia state capital.

1880: Move over, Savannah! With a population of more than 37,000, Atlanta became the state's largest city.

At Sweetwater Creek State Park, visitors can see remains of a cotton mill burned during the Civil War.

John Pemberton

1886: Atlanta officials passed a law prohibiting the sale of alcohol. In response, local pharmacist John Pemberton introduced a drink he had developed: Coca-Cola.

1895: An important leader in the Black community, Booker T. Washington, gave a speech at a conference in Atlanta. He encouraged Black people to focus on getting good jobs, and not to try for social and racial equality with white people. Many community leaders, both Black and white, approved of the idea at the time, but it later became unpopular. W.E.B. DuBois, another Black leader, criticized Washington's idea as the "Atlanta Compromise" because Black people were being told to give in. He encouraged Black people to fight for full equality with white people.

Booker T. Washington

History: Atlanta Grows Up

Early 1900s: "Jim Crow" laws were passed in Atlanta and Georgia. These laws permitted segregation and other ways of discriminating against Black people. The state created separate facilities for Black people, including schools, bathrooms, pools, and more.

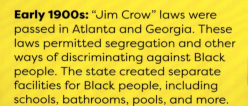

1906: White people attacked African Americans and their businesses in a race riot that killed at least two dozen people. Afterward, African Americans rebuilt in a new community, Sweet Auburn. It became a successful district for Black-run businesses.

1917: The Great Atlanta Fire burned for ten hours in central Atlanta and destroyed more than 1,900 buildings. It was the city's worst fire since the Civil War.

By 1950, Atlanta was home to more than 600,000 people; the city's downtown continued to grow upward.

1936: Atlanta author Margaret Mitchell published *Gone With the Wind*, a hugely popular novel set in the South during the Civil War. It was turned into a movie in 1939. It won the Academy Award (Oscar) for Best Picture of the Year.

1946: The Communicable Disease Center (CDC) was founded in Atlanta with the goal of preventing malaria. It later expanded into the Centers for Disease Control and Prevention, and is now a major agency devoted to public health.

1949: WERD, the first African-American-owned radio station began broadcasting.

History: Civil Rights in Atlanta

By the 1950s, Black people in the South were starting to push back more forcefully against racist Jim Crow laws and segregation. Racial conflicts occurred in many parts of the United States, but in the early days of the movement, Atlanta was fairly quiet. Focused on economic growth, Mayor William Hartsfield called it "the city too busy to hate." That was false.

1957: Atlanta native Dr. Martin Luther King Jr. and other leaders created the Southern Christian Leadership Council and based it in Atlanta. The SCLC became an important voice in the growing Civil Rights Movement.

1950s and 1960s: As the Civil Rights Movement grew, Black and white Atlantans saw more conflicts. Led by Dr. King, (see page 28), the city became a focal point for the nationwide Civil Rights Movement, fighting for equality for Black citizens.

1960: Students from Morehouse College joined together to fight segregation, leading protests and sit-ins across the city. It was the start of the "Atlanta Student Movement." One of the leaders, Julian Bond, later became a US Congressman.

August 30, 1961: Atlanta public schools became officially integrated when nine African American high-school students successfully went to schools that formerly had been only for white students.

1966: After white police shot an unarmed Black man, residents in the Black neighborhood of Summerhill took to the streets to protest. When police showed up to stop them, fights broke out and spread to nearby neighborhoods.

1973: Maynard Jackson was elected as the city's first Black mayor.

History: New Directions

1962: A plane crash in Paris, France, killed 106 arts supporters who had been visiting from Atlanta. The money raised after the crash went to establish new museums and theaters in Atlanta. This is the High Museum of Art.

1974: Playing for the Atlanta Braves in front of a sold-out hometown crowd, Hank Aaron hit his 715th home run, breaking the longstanding record by Babe Ruth.

1980: Businessman Ted Turner launched Cable News Network, better known as CNN.

1996: The city hosted the Summer Olympic Games.

2005: Hartsfield-Jackson International Airport became the world's busiest airport for passenger flights. It remained No. 1 every year but one through 2022. (In 2020, during the COVID-19 pandemic, Guangzhou Baiyun International Airport in China was No. 1.)

2005: Development began on the Atlanta BeltLine.

People from the Past!

People from Atlanta have been making an impact on the world for years. Here are some you should know!

Emily Fitten McDougald (1849-1938): In the early 1900s, women could not vote in most elections. Emily McDougald worked to change that, writing letters, talking to lawmakers, and passing out pamphlets. In 1920, the country passed the 19th amendment to the Constitution, giving women the right to vote.

Dorothy Bolden (1923-2005): Bolden was nine years old when she started to work as a domestic worker. It was a hard job and did not pay much. Most domestic workers were Black women working for white families. Bolden helped organize a union for domestic workers. It helped workers get better pay and working conditions.

Henry "Hank" Aaron (1934-2021):
Aaron was a professional baseball player for the Atlanta Braves. His nickname was "Hammerin' Hank" because he was so good at hitting home runs. In 1974, he hit the 715th home run of his career. It broke the longstanding record held by Babe Ruth. It was also news that a Black player playing in the South topped the record of a white player. Today, Aaron is considered one of the greatest baseball players of all time.

John Lewis (1940-2020):
John Lewis worked alongside Dr. Martin Luther King Jr., during the 1960s Civil Rights movement. In 1986, Lewis was elected to Congress, representing Atlanta, and he continued his fight for equality. In 2011, President Barack Obama awarded Lewis the Presidential Medal of Freedom for his contributions to the country.

The Home of Dr. King

The United States' most famous civil rights activist was Dr. Martin Luther King Jr. He was born in Atlanta and called the city home for most of his life.

King was born in Atlanta in 1929. He was an exceptional student and entered Morehouse College in Atlanta at age 15. He graduated in 1948. He decided to become a minister and headed to Montgomery, Alabama, where he became pastor of Dexter Avenue Baptist Church.

King married Coretta Scott, a singer, in 1953. She became an important civil rights activist, too.

FAST FACT
A boycott is refusing to do or buy something, as a way of protesting.

In 1955 King helped organize the Montgomery Bus Boycott after the arrest of Rosa Parks (pictured). African Americans refused to ride city buses as a way of protesting segregation on buses (Black passengers were nearly always forced to sit in the back of the bus, while white passengers rode up front). Later that year, King earned a doctorate in theology from Boston University.

Dr. King moved back to Atlanta and became a pastor at Ebenezer Baptist Church in 1960.

FAST FACT
In 1960 Dr. King was arrested during a protest and went to jail. He would later be arrested at least 29 more times while fighting for equality.

Throughout the 1960s, Dr. King helped organize more protests against racial segregation, including the March on Washington in 1963, and the march from Selma, Alabama, to Montgomery, Alabama, in 1965.

In 1964, Dr. King was awarded the Nobel Peace Prize in honor of his lifelong work for equal rights and his call for nonviolent resistance.

In 1968, Dr. King was assassinated by a white man, James Earl Ray, in Memphis, Tennessee. His funeral was held in Atlanta, where he is now buried.

The King Center
In 1968, Coretta Scott King created the The Martin Luther King Jr. Center for Nonviolent Social Change, which is still very active today, still very active today, working to educate millions about equal rights for all people.

Atlanta 29

ATLANTA NEIGHBORHOODS

Atlanta is a big city—with a lot of small neighborhoods. They all have their own personalities.

Downtown Atlanta is where you'll find skyscrapers, hotels, businesses, and the state capitol building. Five streets meet in the center at **Five Points**. It's on the site of a trail created by indigenous people hundreds of years ago.

Midtown is separate from Downtown, and is generally the area around and near Pioneer Park.

As the home of Martin Luther King, Jr., the **Old Fourth Ward** represents the center of the 1960s Civil Rights Movement. There's more African-American history just to the south in **Sweet Auburn**, one of the first areas where Black-owned businesses thrived.

Today, African-American culture also thrives in neighborhoods like **West End** and **Castleberry Hill**.

Virginia-Highland and **Little Five Points** are known for quirky shops and restaurants. It's easy to spend the day strolling around. **Buckhead**, in northern Atlanta, has more upscale shopping and art galleries.

You can check out amazing Victorian homes in **Inman Park**, which was established in 1890 and is Atlanta's oldest neighborhood.

. . . and Beyond! Atlanta has dozens of suburbs like **Druid Hills**, **Decatur**, **Marietta**, and **South Fulton**.

Why Is It So Hot and Sticky? Weather in Atlanta

It's no secret the summer weather in Atlanta can get uncomfortably hot, but it's not *always* that way. Plan a trip that isn't in the dog days of summer and you'll be fine. Or, just put on shorts, sip on a cold drink, and make the best of it!

Atlanta's humid, subtropical climate means it's hot and wet (or at least wet-ish) for most of the year. The city gets about 50 inches of rain each year, most of it between December and April.

Especially in July and August, air conditioning is your friend. Daytime high temperatures can climb into the 90s. The humidity makes it feel much hotter. It's typical weather for the South, but, hey, it could be worse: Atlanta's high elevation helps cool things off a bit.

FAST FACTS
Climate means what the weather is like over long periods of time each year. **Weather** means what it's like outside right now.

Kids can cool off on the Olympic-ring-shaped fountain at Centennial Park.

Does it ever get cold? Sure, but don't expect a snow day. Atlanta gets only a couple of inches of snow each year. Ice storms are actually more likely! So maybe an "Ice Day?"

Up here! One of the best ways to see the park—and the city—is from **Skyview Atlanta**, a 20-story-high Ferris wheel.

Things to see in Atlanta

Atlanta is packed with interesting sites, fun activities, and places to explore. Let's look at the most popular!

Centennial Olympic Park

In 1996, the modern Olympic Games celebrated its centennial, or 100th anniversary—and Atlanta was the city where it all happened. After hosting the Games, the city of Atlanta turned the sports site into Centennial Olympic Park. It's a 22-acre park full of art, sculptures, and green space.

Perfect for a selfie: Five overlapping colored rings are the logo of the Olympics. Here you can see a giant sculpture of the rings named "The Spectacular." How spectacular? They're 11 feet tall, 23 feet long, and 5,000 pounds heavy. You can also see the rings on the Fountain of Rings (page 32-33). On hot days, kids (and grown-ups) can splash around in more than 250 water jets that squirt 35 feet high! There's a show four times daily when the jets are choreographed to music and lights.

Things to See in Atlanta

Take the ultimate taste test at the **World of Coca-Cola**. You can trace the history of the famous soft drink, taste different Coke beverages from around the world, and even experiment with your own concoctions. Then, go inside the vault where the secret recipe is kept—but don't get too excited; they won't let you see it!

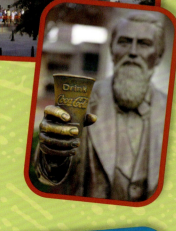

Shop til you Drop: **Atlantic Station** is a huge complex of stores, condominiums, and art galleries northwest of Midtown. If you're looking for something unique, try the **Junkman's Daughter** in Little Five Points, which is stuffed with books, clothes, knickknacks, and tons of other offbeat stuff.

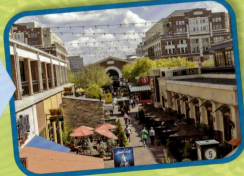

Walk through the treetops at the **Atlanta Botanical Garden** in Piedmont Park. The Canopy Walk puts guests 40 feet (12 m) in the air where they can look down on the gardens below. There's an old-growth forest, a rose garden, and exhibits of plants from different ecosystems, like rainforests and deserts. There's even a Children's Garden just for kids.

See what it's like to sit behind the desk of a news broadcast at the **CNN Center**. You'll get a behind-the-scenes look at what goes on, and see the technology used to make weather maps and other graphics. Want to try it out yourself? You can also get a video made while you're reading the day's headlines.

FAST FACT
Save money with a **CityPASS**, which gets you into several attractions at a discount.

Atlanta 37

Things to See in Atlanta

Let mom and dad eat and shop on the ground floor of Ponce City Market, then drag them upstairs to **Skyline Park** on the roof. There, you can play arcade and carnival games like skee ball and mini golf, travel up a cable on Heege Tower for great views of the city, and slide down a three-story slide.

For even more thrilling thrills, drive thirty minutes west of Atlanta to **Six Flags Over Georgia**, which has all the roller coasters you could want.

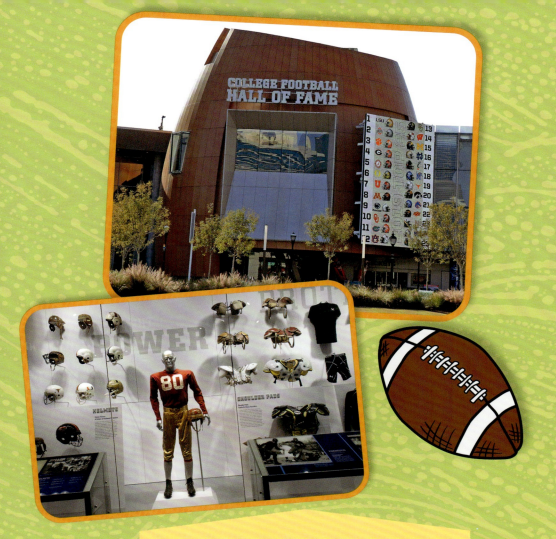

What is a fall Saturday for? In the South, the answer is college football! At the **College Football Hall of Fame** you can discover the history of the game, find out more about players and coaches from your favorite teams, and relive some of the cooler moments from over the decades. Feeling restless? Shake it out at the "Skill Zone" by testing out your throwing arm and kicking a field goal. You can even record your own play-by-play broadcast and design a mascot.

Atlanta

Things to See in Atlanta

Atlanta has been called the "cradle of the Civil Rights movement." Thousands of citizens here, both Black and white, marched, protested and spoke out about racial injustice and inequality. Here's where to find out more.

At the **Martin Luther King, Jr. Historical Park** in downtown Atlanta, you can tour King's childhood home, see Ebenezer Baptist Church where he preached, and learn more about his life and work at the King Center.

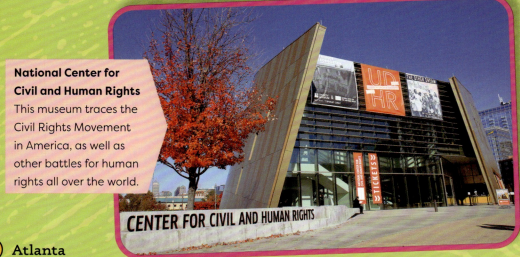

National Center for Civil and Human Rights
This museum traces the Civil Rights Movement in America, as well as other battles for human rights all over the world.

Sweet Auburn

This Atlanta neighborhood has long been a center of Black life.

A local businessman called the area around **Auburn Avenue** "sweet" because African American businesses thrived there in the early 1900s. Several historical homes, businesses, and churches are still there.

The **Madame C.J. Walker Museum** honors this successful Black businesswoman. She was the first Black millionaire thanks to her hair products business. The same building also was home to WERD, a black-owned radio station, plus Dr. King's office.

Congressman John Lewis was an Atlanta legend. Next to the Curb Market is a huge mural of him. "Hero" painted atop it shows how important he was to the city.

Hungry? The **Sweet Auburn Curb Market** is a farmers' market that's more than 100 years old. In the old days, only white sellers were allowed inside—but Black vendors could do business outside, at the curb. The nickname stuck.

Atlanta

STONE MOUNTAIN

About an hour west of Atlanta stands Stone Mountain. Though if you want to be exact, you'll need to call Stone "Mountain" a quartz monzonite monadnock. Say that three times fast and we're guessing you'll be back to "stone mountain." The giant pile of rock is in a huge park that is popular with visitors and offers lots of things to do and see.

What is a monadnock? Pretty much what it looks like: a large rock hill that sticks out from the surrounding area.

In the 1800s, the mountain was a giant quarry where workers mined granite to use in construction projects.

The monadnock was formed about 15 million years ago, when underground magma bubbled up to the surface, and cooled to form granite.

42 Atlanta

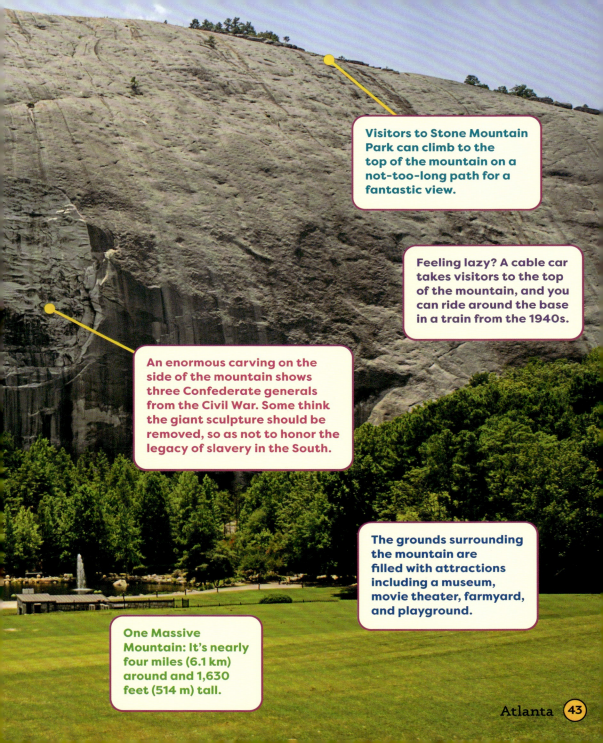

Visitors to Stone Mountain Park can climb to the top of the mountain on a not-too-long path for a fantastic view.

Feeling lazy? A cable car takes visitors to the top of the mountain, and you can ride around the base in a train from the 1940s.

An enormous carving on the side of the mountain shows three Confederate generals from the Civil War. Some think the giant sculpture should be removed, so as not to honor the legacy of slavery in the South.

The grounds surrounding the mountain are filled with attractions including a museum, movie theater, farmyard, and playground.

One Massive Mountain: It's nearly four miles (6.1 km) around and 1,630 feet (514 m) tall.

Atlanta

GETTING AROUND ATLANTA

The easiest way to get around Atlanta is by car. But a lot of the most popular places are concentrated in the city center, and there are more options for reaching those.

The Metropolitan Atlanta Rapid Transit Authority (MARTA) is a system of buses and trains that go all around the city and its outlying regions. You can buy a single trip or a multi-day pass.

That's Just Peachy

Peachtree Street is one of the most important streets in Atlanta, but make sure you don't get it confused with Peachtree Road, Peachtree Lane, Peachtree Circle, Peachtree Walk, Peachtree Place . . . are you getting the idea? There are more than 70 streets in Atlanta with the word "Peachtree," so read your directions carefully!

If you're right in the middle of Atlanta, go retro with a ride on the Atlanta Streetcar. It covers a 2.7 mile (4.3 km) loop between Martin Luther King Jr. National Historic Site and Centennial Olympic Park, with 10 stops along the way.

Try some sweat-powered transportation by using one of the city's shareable bikes or scooters. Pay a small rental fee to pick it up at one of the stations located throughout the city, and return it to any station you want.

Atlanta 45

Art in Atlanta

Hands On! The **ATL playground** in Woodruff Park is the best in artful fun. Slides, monkey bars, and a climbing wall are all built into this ultimate Atlanta sculpture.

A steel sculpture honors Dr. Martin Luther King. **"Homage to King"** is a steel sculpture on Freedom Parkway that shows him speaking to an audience, his arm raised in the air.

Atlanta

Graffiti covers every square inch of **Krog Street Tunnel** between Inman Park and Cabbagetown. Some of it is murals and street art; some of it is words and messages. There have even been marriage proposals spray-painted there!

Local artist **Karen Anderson Singer** thinks small—tiny, actually. She makes miniature doors only seven inches tall, and installs them all over the city. They're decorated to reflect their surroundings.

Murals throughout the city celebrate street art, the outdoor world, and just plain wacky stuff, depending on where you are. There's way more than we can list here, but you can get an app for a driving tour of murals and other street art .

Atlanta

High Museum of Art The High gets its name from an Atlanta family who donated their home to display works held by the Atlanta Art Association. This museum is part of the Woodruff Arts Center, a major performance and visual arts museum in the Southeast. The High has works by famous artists like Rembrandt and Picasso.

Check out African American artists at **Clark Atlanta University Art Museum**. The **Spelman College Museum of Fine Art** showcases work by Black women artists.

Get a fresh take on art at the **Atlanta Contemporary Art Center**, which features local, national, and international artists in always-changing exhibits. Plus, this museum is always free.

There are more than 17,000 ancient artifacts from Greece, Rome, Egypt, Africa, and the Americas at the **Michael C. Carlos Museum**. The museum began at Emory University way back in 1876.

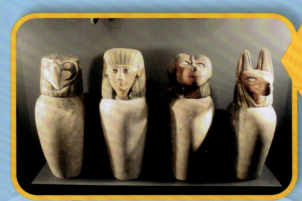

Art, photography, and other items are on display at the **APEX Museum**, which preserves African culture and history.

Everything from skateboards to showers can be the focus at the **Museum of Design Atlanta** (MODA). Exhibits on architecture, interior design and furniture, clothing, and graphic design are some of the highlights.

Atlanta

Other Great Atlanta Museums

Museums are great for more than art, of course. Atlanta has something for just about everyone!

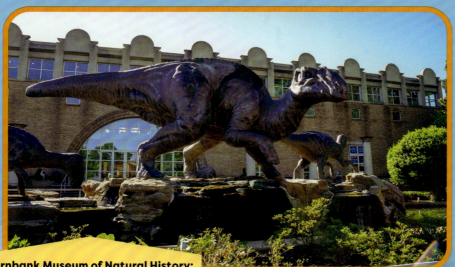

Fernbank Museum of Natural History: Of course there's all the usual "museum stuff." But there's also a 75-acre forest, a 3D theater, and live animals! Check out dinosaur models, take a "walk through time in Georgia," and learn what's happening in science today.

Atlanta History Center: Learn about Native Americans in Georgia, the history of Atlanta's railroads, the Civil War, and more. This cool museum has lots of artifacts, plus music, oral histories, and even computer games!

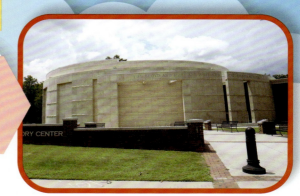

Margaret Mitchell House: Mitchell lived here while she wrote her epic (and only) novel, *Gone With the Wind*. Although popular, the book was also criticized for not accurately describing the Civil War and slavery. The museum here explores these ideas, and their role in history.

Two for One: The museum at the State Capitol building has the stuffed heads of a two-headed cow on display, along with a two-headed snake. The collection also includes a number of other odd artifacts.

At the **Delta Flight Museum**, complete a scavenger hunt as you learn about aviation history, see antique planes, and go inside a massive, two-deck Boeing 747.

Atlanta

Performing Arts

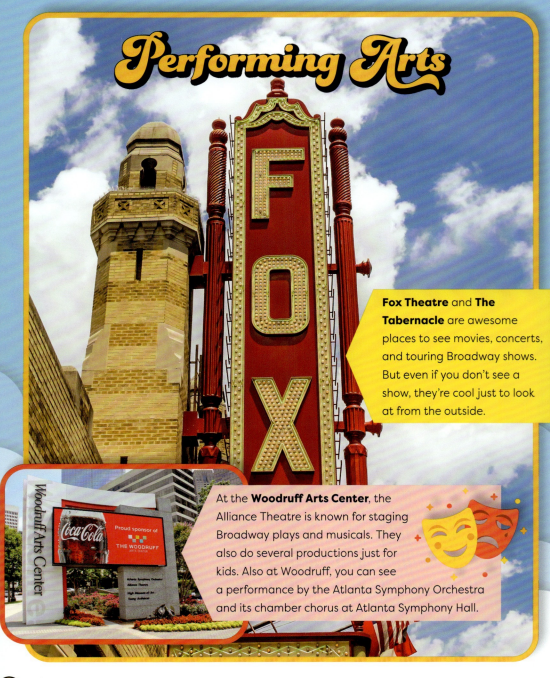

Fox Theatre and **The Tabernacle** are awesome places to see movies, concerts, and touring Broadway shows. But even if you don't see a show, they're cool just to look at from the outside.

At the **Woodruff Arts Center**, the Alliance Theatre is known for staging Broadway plays and musicals. They also do several productions just for kids. Also at Woodruff, you can see a performance by the Atlanta Symphony Orchestra and its chamber chorus at Atlanta Symphony Hall.

 **Atlanta Ballet**, founded in 1929, is the oldest continuously operating ballet company in the country. The company's main performance space is the Cobb Energy Performing Arts Centre.

 Catch a movie at the **Starlight Six Drive-In**, or check out one of the many free outdoor films offered during the summer.

 The **Center for Puppetry Arts** is one of the largest puppet museums in the world, with puppets from Jim Henson's Muppets as well as other collections. The center also offers puppet-making classes, and puts on performances throughout the year for kids and teens.

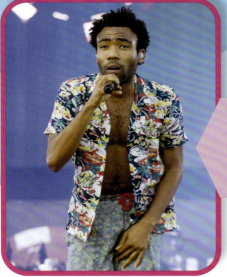 **One Really Hip Place** If you're a hip-hop fan, Atlanta is the place to be. A form of rap music, Southern rap, took hold here in the 1980s. Popular artists like T.I., Jeezy, Ludacris, Childish Gambino (pictured), and OutKast all got their start here.

Atlanta

How to Talk Atlanta

You want to blend in with the other six million folks in Atlanta, right? Then talk the talk of a true Atlantan!

Walk a Dog
Getting a hot dog to go from Atlanta's famous Varsity restaurant.

Spaghetti Junction
This is a nickname for a place where a lot of freeways in Atlanta all twist up with each other. It's in the northern part of the city.

The Hooch
Nickname for the local river, the Chattahoochee. You "Shoot the Hooch" by taking a kayak or inner tube down the river.

Goobers
The ATL name for peanuts!

ATL
The name of the town! Just saying ATL tells people where you are. A-Town is good, too. What's *not* cool is "Hotlanta"— that's for tourists only!

ITP/OTP
In or out? The I-285 freeway circles Atlanta, forming a perimeter, or border. If you're inside, you're ITP (inside the perimeter). Guess what OTP means?

ATLANTA: It's Weird!

Constitution Lakes Park used to be the site of a brick company. When it became a park, a local carpenter started making art from old doll parts and other trash on the site. He displayed it in the park, leading to **Doll's Head Trail**.

Wait, this book is not about Washington, DC, So what is the White House doing in here? Well, Atlanta has one, too. Developer Fred Milani built it in the late 1990s. It has an Oval Office just like the real White House. You can only look from the outside, though, since it's now a private family home.

Whatever you do, don't sit down at this museum in Stone Mountain. You'll crush one of the exhibits at the **Museum of Miniature Chairs**. Owner Barbara Hartsfield owns more than 3,000 tiny chairs and displays many of them at her museum/gift shop.

Got plans on May 28, 8113? If you're around, head to Atlanta for the opening of a time capsule at Oglethorpe University. The university president came up with the idea in the 1930s, and it's actually an entire sealed room stuffed with books, toys, tools, clothing, household items, and pretty much everything else.

Visit the Atlanta State Capitol museum to check out this bizarre stuffed two-headed cow and see other oddities. There's also a two-headed snake. The museum has lots of interesting non-weird stuff, too!

The baseball stadium where Hank Aaron hit his historic 715th home run, breaking Babe Ruth's longstanding record, was demolished in 1997. Now the place is a parking lot. But you can't demolish history. The piece of the fence where the ball went over it was left in place.

Hey! I'm from Atlanta too!

Chloe Grace Moretz

Actress, Born in Atlanta on February 10, 1997

Moretz grew up with four older brothers, so she knows how to make herself stand out. The family moved to New York City when Chloe was five and one of her brothers went to school for acting. Moretz helped him practice, and ended up going into acting herself. She's been in lots of movies and TV shows and is an advocate for LGBTQ rights.

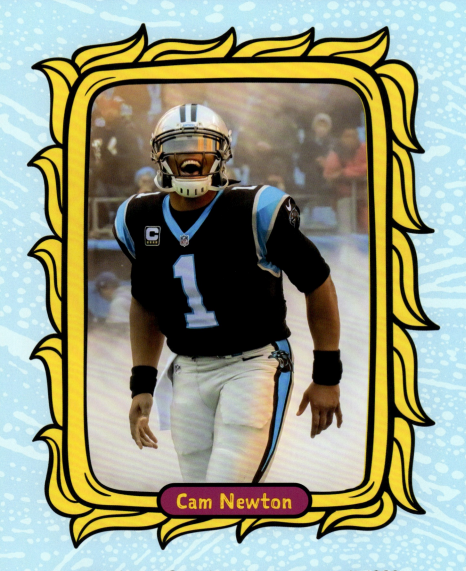

Cam Newton

NFL player, Born in Atlanta on May 11, 1989

Football fans know all about Newton, who has played quarterback for the Carolina Panthers and the New England Patriots. In 2010, he won the Heisman Trophy, which is awarded to the best player in college football. As a pro he has received the Most Valuable Player (MVP) award. He holds a league record for rushing touchdowns by a quarterback.

What People Do IN ATLANTA

Atlanta's a busy place—it's the biggest city in between Houston and Miami, and still growing. Here's a look at what keeps Atlanta going:

Transportation is a big industry in the city that's always moving. It's got the headquarters for major corporations like Delta Airlines and UPS. Plus it's got the busiest airport in the world, helping move people and packages all over the globe.

Major research hospitals and universities like Emory, and government health agencies like the CDC, make Atlanta a healthcare hub of the Southeast.

Coca-Cola sells almost two billion drinks every day around the world. Thousands of people work at the Coke company headquarters here so folks can get their fix.

Fintech is short for "financial technology," and Atlanta rules this industry. From credit card payments to cryptocurrency, about 70 percent of the world's sales pass through Atlanta using one of its fintech companies.

Speaking of fixing, when you need a job done, you might take a trip to Home Depot. The company's headquarters are located here, and it's one of the city's—and the state's—largest employers.

HOLLYWOOD of the South

You've probably seen parts of Atlanta on TV and in the movies. In the last ten years it's gotten the nickname "Hollywood of the South." With almost 500 movies a year filmed here, there are actually more made in Georgia than in Hollywood!

Why here? Back in the early 2000s, the Georgia government convinced TV producers and filmmakers to come to the state by giving them big tax breaks. That made it much less expensive to make some movies or TV shows.

And . . . action! Big-budget action movies like *Ant-Man and the Wasp*, *Avengers: Infinity War*, *Spiderman: Homecoming*, and *Captain America: Civil War* have used Atlanta-area locations.

That's horrible! A lot of horror, zombie, and apocalypse movies and TV shows have been made in Atlanta, like *The Walking Dead*, *The Hunger Games*, *The Vampire Diaries*, and *Stranger Things*.

Actor and filmmaker **Tyler Perry** moved to Atlanta when he was 22 to start his entertainment career. He opened Tyler Perry Studios in Atlanta in 2015.

FAST FACT
Just south of the city is Trilith Studios, the largest production facility in the state. It covers 700 acres and has 24 soundstages!

The next generation of producers, lighting and set designers, makeup artists, and more can learn their trade at the **Georgia Film Academy**, opened in 2015.

Atlanta

Eat the Atlanta Way

Atlanta is a great place to eat, whether you like food from around the world, farmers' markets, or Southern cooking. Check out some of these Atlanta faves:

Atlantans have developed their own flavor of chicken wings: lemon pepper. You can find them at restaurants throughout Atlanta; **J.R. Crickets** is one good choice.

When it's hot, cool down with an ice pop from **King of Pops**, a local business with carts all around the city.

The South is about soul food, and there are some great places in Atlanta for fried chicken, catfish, black-eyed peas, fried green tomatoes, collard greens, cornbread, peach cobbler, and more. Local favorites include **Paschal's**, **The Busy Bee**, and **Mary Mac's Tea Room**.

Doughnut wars? If you want to show some loyalty to the city, grab the A-Town cream from **Sublime Doughnuts**. The flavors are the same as a Boston cream doughnut, but in the shape of an A. You might also luck out at **Revolution Doughnuts**, which serves peach sliders—a sugar doughnut filled with peaches—when the fruit's in season.

Taking up two blocks, the **Varsity** is the largest drive-in restaurant in the world (but you can eat inside, too.) Chili cheese hot dogs are the main attraction here, and don't forget a side of onion rings.

Atlanta 65

Go, Atlanta Sports!

Atlanta is home to some awesome pro sports teams. Go, team, go!

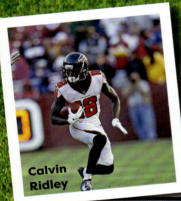
Calvin Ridley

ATLANTA FALCONS

Joined the National Football League in 1965.

Won Two NFC championships (1998 and 2016), sending them to the Super Bowl, (which they lost both times).

Famous for the "Dirty Bird" touchdown dance made popular by running back Jamal Anderson in 1998. Fans still do the dance today!

Big Names: Deion Sanders, Steve Bartkowski, Andre Rison, Jamal Anderson, Matt Ryan, Tommy Nobis

Home: Mercedes-Benz Stadium

ATLANTA BRAVES

Joined professional baseball in 1871 in Boston; moved to Milwaukee in 1953; moved to Atlanta in 1966

Won the World Series in 1914, 1957, 1995, and 2021

Big Names: Hank Aaron, Warren Spahn, Chipper Jones, Greg Maddux, Andruw Jones, Ronald Acuña

Home: Truist Park

Can't get enough baseball? Check out a game with the minor league Gwinnett Stripers (named for striped bass fish).

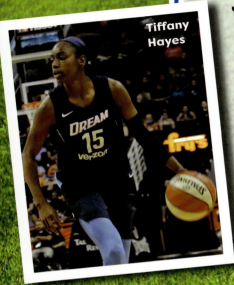
Tiffany Hayes

ATLANTA DREAM

Joined the Women's National Basketball Association in 2008.

Won conference championships in 2010, 2011, and 2013

The team name was chosen to honor Martin Luther King Jr.'s famous "I Have a Dream" speech

Big Names: Angel McCoughtry, Chennedy Carter, Erika De Souza, Sancho Lyttle, Courtney Williams

Home: Gateway Center Arena

ATLANTA HAWKS

Joined what became the NBA in 1946; moved to Atlanta in 1968

Won the league championship in 1958, but not since then.

Famous for being one of the first teams in the NBA

Big Names: Dominique Wilkins, Trae Young, Bob Pettit, "Pistol" Pete Maravich

Home: State Farm Arena

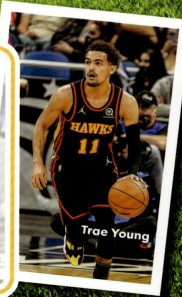
Trae Young

ATLANTA UNITED FC

Team founded in 2014; joined Major League Soccer in 2017;

Won the US Open Cup in 2019 and 2022, and the MLS Cup in 2018

Before games, players sign a "golden spike" to honor the city's railroad history, and a VIP guest hammers it into a platform

Big Names: Josef Martinez, Miguel Almiron, Hector Villalba, Michael Parkhurst, Jeff Larentowicz

Home: Mercedes-Benz Stadium

Until it was topped by Charlotte in 2021, Atlanta United had the MLS record for attendance at a game with more than 72,000 people!

Join In!

Take advantage of Atlanta's warm weather and acres of outdoor space to have some fun yourself!

Get wet and shoot the Hooch! Take a raft, inner tube, or kayak down the **Chattahoochee River**. The river's pretty tame in metro Atlanta, although rapids can get more intense in stretches farther away. Be sure to wear a life jacket—it's the law for people 13 and under.

When the skate park in **Fourth Ward Park** opened in 2011, champion skateboarder Tony Hawk gave it a whirl. This huge, world-class park offers ramps, rails, bowls, ledges, and lots of ups and downs. Just starting out? There's some easier places. On the advanced side? You're covered. Hey, if it was good enough for Tony . . .

Runner Up! Over the July Fourth holiday, 60,000 people run in the **Peachtree Road Race**. It's the largest 10K race in the world!

Take it slower with a hike on one of Atlanta's dozens of urban trails. The Palisades Trail along the Chattahoochee River has two sections: The West side is paved, and a little easier, while the East side is a bit more challenging. Another good bet is the two-mile loop trail at **Cascade Springs Nature Preserve**. You'll be rewarded with an overlook view and a waterfall along the way.

COLLEGE TOWN

With more than 40 colleges and universities in Atlanta, you can earn a degree in any subject you want!

GEORGIA INSTITUTE OF TECHNOLOGY (GEORGIA TECH)

Founded 1885
Students: 27,000
Popular majors: Computer science, Mechanical engineering, Business, Aerospace and Aeronautical engineering, Biomedical engineering, Electronics
Fast Fact: Freshmen can run in the half-mile "cake race" held on Homecoming weekend. They get a cupcake at the end.

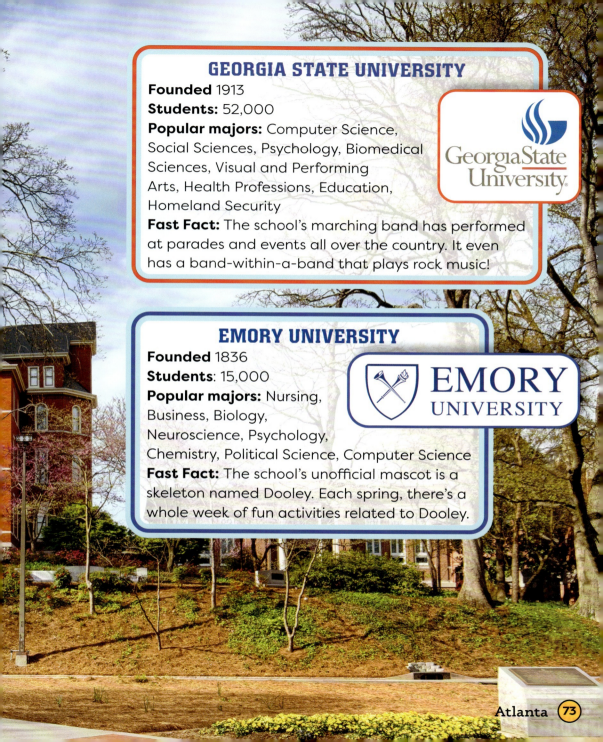

GEORGIA STATE UNIVERSITY

Founded 1913
Students: 52,000
Popular majors: Computer Science, Social Sciences, Psychology, Biomedical Sciences, Visual and Performing Arts, Health Professions, Education, Homeland Security
Fast Fact: The school's marching band has performed at parades and events all over the country. It even has a band-within-a-band that plays rock music!

EMORY UNIVERSITY

Founded 1836
Students: 15,000
Popular majors: Nursing, Business, Biology, Neuroscience, Psychology, Chemistry, Political Science, Computer Science
Fast Fact: The school's unofficial mascot is a skeleton named Dooley. Each spring, there's a whole week of fun activities related to Dooley.

Atlanta

Atlanta's HBCUs

HBCU stands for Historically Black Colleges and Universities. Atlanta University Center is home to several important HBCUs.

CLARK ATLANTA UNIVERSITY

Founded: 1865
Students: 2,500
Popular Majors: Business, marketing, communications, psychology, visual arts.
Fast Fact: Atlanta University was founded by a pair of formerly enslaved men right after the Civil War. It merged in 1869 with Clark, a Methodist school also focused on Black students.

The Kilgore Center is for students at Morehouse College.

MOREHOUSE SCHOOL OF MEDICINE

Founded: 1975
Students: 350
Popular Majors: Medicine
Fast Fact: MSM, as it's known, became a separate co-ed medical graduate school in 1981.

MOREHOUSE COLLEGE

Founded: 1867
Students: 2,200
Popular Majors:
Fast Fact: A school for men only, Morehouse has dozens of famous alumni, including Dr. Martin Luther King, Jr., former Atlanta mayor Maynard Jackson, Senator Raphael Warnock, film director Spike Lee, and actor Samuel L. Jackson.

SPELMAN COLLEGE

Founded: 1881
Students: 2,400
Popular Majors: Biological sciences, English, physical science, psychology
Fast Fact: A college for women only, it began as a training school for Baptist ministers. By the 1960s, its students were playing a key role in the Civil Rights movement.

HBCU History: For many years in America it was very hard for a Black person to attend college. Because of segregation (rules and laws that kept Black and white people separate), college was mostly just a dream. Cheyney College, the first school of higher education for Black students was founded in 1837 in Pennsylvania. In the years after the Civil War, many more HBCUs were founded and today there are more than 100. All of them give thousands of Black students—and students from many backgrounds—a chance at top college and university degrees.

Atlanta

It's Alive! Animals in Atlanta

Georgia has a ton of wildlife, from alligators in the swamps to birds in the trees. Most wildlife in Atlanta is of the human kind, but if you keep your eyes open you might see some of these animals, too:

Deer

You probably won't see a **black bear** in downtown Atlanta, but as the city pushes north into forested areas, it's more common to come into contact with one.

Fox

Atlanta's skyscrapers are home to more than just businesspeople at work. **Peregrine falcons** are used to nesting in cliffs, so they fit in on the tall buildings just fine.

Red-shouldered hawk

The rivers and lakes in the Atlanta area are home to snapping turtles, Great Blue Herons, and fish like **largemouth bass**, sunfish, and catfish.

We Saw it at the Zoo

Crowd-pleasing animals like gorillas and giant pandas are the stars at **Zoo Atlanta**. The zoo got its start back in 1889, when a local businessman bought some circus animals, including a bear, a jaguar, a hyena, some monkeys and camels, and a few other animals. Now there are about 1,500 animals and more than 200 species!

Visit **Trader's Alley** to learn about species that have been hurt by poaching and illegal wildlife trading. Some of the featured animals are tigers, sun bears, and Asian turtles.

Lemur

Sun bear

Giant pandas

Atlanta is one of only a handful of US zoos with pandas on parade. A pair of giant pandas, Lun Lun and Yang Yang, arrived in Atlanta in 1999, on loan from China. They've since given birth to several cubs.

See what it's like to stroll through Africa in the **Ford African Rain Forest**, which is home to gorillas, lemurs, monkeys, and birds that are native to central Africa. Nearby, elephants, giraffes, lions, zebras, and other grassland-dwellers roam on the **African Savanna** exhibit.

Giraffes

Lions

Another Animal Adventure

For more animal adventures, take a trip to the **Atlanta Alpaca Treehouse**. You can feed carrots to a farm full of llamas and alpacas, learn more about the animals, and check out an awesome treehouse built in the middle of a bamboo forest.

We saw it at the Aquarium

Whales! Sharks! Whale sharks! Plus bottlenose dolphins, sea lions, manta rays, penguins and puffins, and gazillions of fish. They're all on display at the **Georgia Aquarium** in Atlanta.

The Aquarium is the largest in the United Sates and the third-largest in the world. All those animals live in 11 million gallons of water!

How many can you find? Go on a scavenger hunt for different species throughout the aquarium with an app on your phone.

That's a lot of teeth: The aquarium has hammerhead sharks, tiger sharks, sand tiger sharks, zebra sharks, silky sharks, and silvertip sharks. Some adventurous visitors even take a dunk in the shark tank!

FAST FACT
The whale sharks at the aquarium are more than 20 feet (6 m) long! Whale sharks are the largest fish alive, even bigger than great white sharks.

Watch the aquarium's pod of bottlenose dolphins give a show on the **Dolphin Coast**, and get an underwater ocean view at **Ocean Voyager**, a 6.3-million gallon tank with whale sharks, manta rays, and thousands of fish.

Tired yet? You can make a reservation to do a sleepover at the aquarium. (You must be at least seven years old, and you must drag an adult with you.)

Atlanta

Parks!

Remember all those trees? Lots of them grow in Atlanta's awesome collection of public parks.

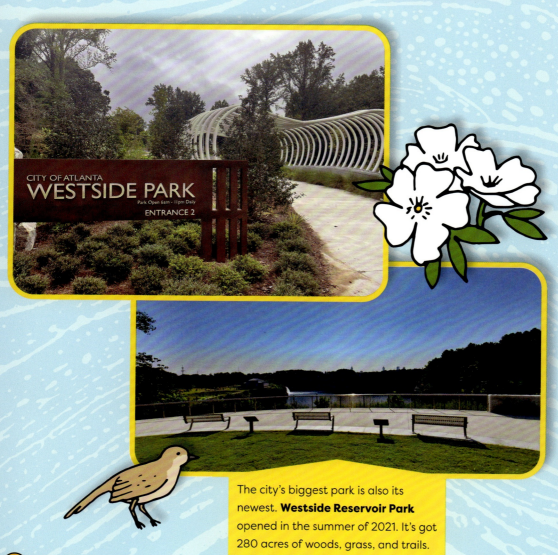

The city's biggest park is also its newest. **Westside Reservoir Park** opened in the summer of 2021. It's got 280 acres of woods, grass, and trails.

There's also plenty of room to stretch out at the 200-acre **Piedmont Park** north of Downtown, home to the Atlanta Botanical Garden. There are playgrounds, picnic areas, and several sports fields. In the summer, cool off in the large pool or hop around on the "splash pad" with water jets that spurt 30 feet (9 m) high. If you're there in winter, you can get in some ice skating.

Hartsfield may be one of the world's busiest airports, but if you want to slow it down, go to **Doc Manget Memorial Aviation Park**. It's next door to DeKalb Peachtree Airport, and you can hang out and watch private jets and small planes take off and land.

Historic **Fourth Ward Park** is packed with great stuff, including a lake, an outdoor theater for concerts, a playground with rock walls and climbing areas, a splashpad, and an extremely cool skatepark (see page 70).

Atlanta

Spooky Sights

Do you believe in ghosts and spirits? Not everyone does . . . but no one knows for sure! Like most cities, Atlanta has lots of places that people say are haunted.

Lots of Atlantans are buried in the old **Oakland Cemetery**, including about 3,000 Confederate soldiers. Visitors sometimes report seeing and hearing the soldiers. One is doing roll call—and getting answers!

In 1946, 119 people died in a fire at the **Winecoff Hotel**, now the **Ellis Hotel**. It's the worst hotel fire in US history. Now, people sometimes see ghosts in the hallways, hear screams, and smell smoke that isn't there. To add to the creepy factor, sometimes the fire alarms go off at 2:48 a.m., the time of the original fire.

In the early 1900s, millionaire **Amos Rhodes** built a mansion in Atlanta. He and his wife died there in the 1920s, but decided to stick around the house. It's now open to visitors who want a glimpse into the past—and possibly of Amos and his wife. People have reported encounters with the couple's ghosts, who are not happy that people are stopping by.

The **Beverly Hills Inn Apartments** in Buckhead was once a home for elderly widows. They definitely did not get the message about Southern hospitality. They float around and whisper "Get out!" to current residents and guests.

Do you smell pipe smoke even though there's no one around? See a fork floating over the table? How about a ghostly boy playing a music box? Then you're likely at **Foster House**, built in 1887 by Henry Foster. Henry and his son died of typhoid fever, but they're still hanging around the house (now a restaurant).

Not Far Away

Atlanta is a big place, but if you've still got some energy, there are a lot of cool places nearby to check out!

> We went to **Athens**!

> In Greece? Seems kind of far away…

> In Georgia. And only about an hour and a half from Atlanta. It was named after the city in Greece, though.

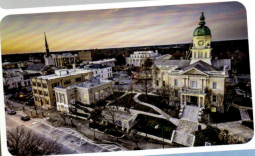

> Is it full of philosophers and fancy architecture?

> Yes and yes. The University of Georgia is here, so it's got that college-town vibe (plus football!). Plus it's the start of the "Antebellum Trail" which are homes from the Civil War. Major fancy.

The **Chattahoochee-Oconee National Forest** is ginormous! It's about half the border with Tennessee.

That's a lot of trees.

And animals. Deer, coyotes, even bears. We were out at dusk and I'm pretty sure I saw some Blue Ghost fireflies. They glow blue, you know.

I kinda guessed that. Did you drive through the whole forest?

No, it's way too big for that. But we did a couple of really pretty drives, and then hiked some. One of my favorite places was **Anna Ruby Falls**. It's an amazing waterfall!

I hope you got pictures.

For sure. Which was way smarter than Mom. SHE got poison ivy!

Atlanta

Not Far Away

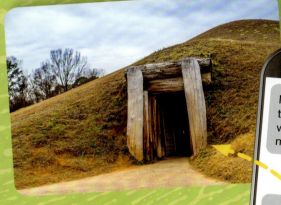

My dad jokes about being alive during the last Ice Age, but the first people who lived here really were. That was more than 10,000 years ago!

Cool! Where are you?

Ocmulgee Mounds National Park, in Macon, Georgia. It's where the largest archaeological dig in US history was made.

Did they find anything good?

Tons. Pottery, weapons, jewelry, all kinds of stuff. 2.5 million artifacts! We saw a lot of it in the museum. But the coolest part is outside. There's a 1,000-year-old Earth Lodge where Native Americans held meetings. Plus the Great Temple Mound, which is 55 feet tall. We climbed to the top.

That sounds hard.

Not for me, but Dad was huffing and puffing. I guess that's what happens when you're thousands of years old. 😀

The **Dahlonega Gold Museum** shows what it was like during Georgia's gold rush. That was back in the 1830s—way before they found gold in California.

> Did you see the mines?

One of them. Consolidated Gold Mine goes 200 feet underground. We walked through the tunnels and saw the old cart rails. There's even an original drill that still works.

> Why don't they use it anymore?

Too hard to get the gold out. Most of what's left is stuck deep in the rocks. It costs more to get it out than it's worth. They showed us how to pan for gold, though. MUCH easier!

> So are you paying next time we go to the movies?

Yep. But not for you!

Sister Cities Around the World

If you think of the world as one big family, it's only natural to think of cities as having sisters. The United States started an official "Sister City" program back in 1956, so people all around the world could get to know each other. Atlanta got its first sister city in 1967, and today it has 17 "ciblings."

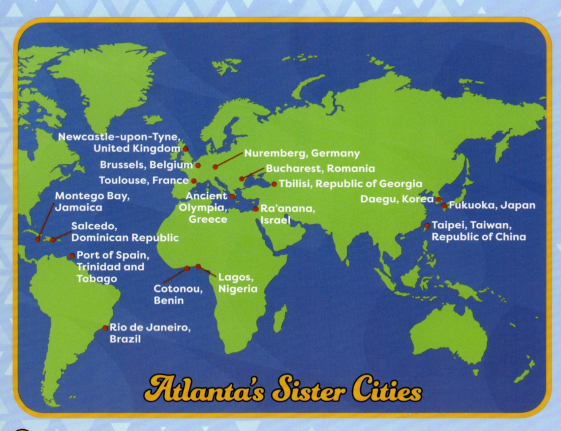

Atlanta's Sister Cities

Here are some things Atlanta is doing with her sister cities:

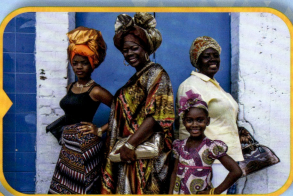

Port of Spain: Atlanta kids got training in soccer with this Caribbean city in Trinidad and Tobago.

Ra'anana: The Daffodil Project is an organization that plants daffodils to remember the 1.5 million children who died during the Holocaust in World War II. In partnership with Ra'anana, the 5K "Daffodil Dash" in Atlanta helps honor those children.

Newcastle and Nuremberg: People from Atlanta's business community have met with folks from England and Germany to build economic ties.

Lagos: Laptops and scholarships have been donated to students in Nigeria.

FIND OUT MORE!
Books, Websites, and More!

Books

Adamson, Heather. *The Civil Rights Movement: An Interactive History Adventure.* Capstone Press, 2016.

Bader, Bonnie. *Who Was Martin Luther King Jr.?* Penguin Workshop, 2007.

Hall, Brianna. *Exploring the Georgia Colony.* Capstone Press, 2016.

Jerome, Kate Boehm. Atlanta, GA: *Cool Stuff Every Kid Should Know.* Arcadia Kids, 2010.

Yomtov, Nel. *Georgia.* Children's Press, 2018.

The Civil War Visual Encyclopedia. DK Children, 2021

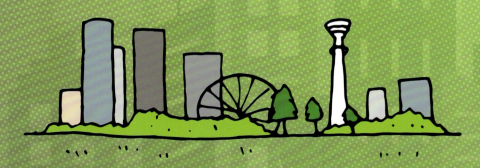

Web Sites

Atlanta Convention & Visitors Bureau
https://discoveratlanta.com/explore/main/

Atlanta BeltLine
https://beltline.org/

Frommer's Travel Guide to Atlanta
https://www.frommers.com/destinations/atlanta/introduction

Secret Atlanta
https://secretatlanta.co/

History of Atlanta for Kids
https://kids.kiddle.co/History_of_Atlanta

African-American Civil Rights Movement, Ducksters
https://www.ducksters.com/history/civil_rights/african-american_civil_rights_movement.php

Photo Credits and Thanks

Photos are from Dreamstime, Shutterstock, or Wikimedia unless otherwise noted. AP Images—AP Photo: 22 BL, 22 TR, 24 BL; 28 TL, 28 CR; 28 BR; Horace Cort: 22 C; Charles Pugh/Atlanta Journal-Constitution: 22 CR; Sadayuki Mikami: 22 BR. Dwight Ross Jr./Atlanta Journal-Constitution: 26 BL; Gene Herrick: 28 C; Focus on Sports—60 B. Atlantaparks.com—72.

Artwork: LemonadePixel. Maps (6-7): Jessica Nevins.

Thanks to our pal Nancy Ellwood, Kait Leggett, and all the fine folks at Arcadia!

INDEX

Aaron, Hank 24, 27, 57, 67
APEX Museum 49
Atlanta Alpaca Treehouse 79
Atlanta Ballet 53
Atlanta BeltLine 12, 13, 25
Atlanta Botanical Garden 37
Atlanta Braves 24, 67
Atlanta Compromise 19
Atlanta Contemporary Art Center 49
Atlanta Dream 68
Atlanta Falcons 66
Atlanta Hawks 68
Atlanta History Center 10, 50
Atlanta United FC 69
Atlanta University 18
Atlantic Station 36
Bolden, Dorothy 26
Bond, Julian 23
Cascade Spring Nature Preserve 71
Centennial Olympic Park 33, 35
Center for Puppetry Arts 53
Chattahoochee-Oconee National Forest 87

Chattahoochee River 15, 54, 70
Cherokee people 15, 17
Civil Rights Movement 22, 23, 27
Civil War 4, 18, 43
Clark Atlanta University 18, 48, 74
Clark Atlanta University Art Museum 48
CNN 25, 37
Coca-Cola 19, 36, 61
College Football Hall of Fame 39
Communicable Disease Center (CDC) 21
Creek people 16
Delta Flight Museum 51
Dexter Avenue Baptist Church 28
Dahlonega Gold Museum 89
Doc Manget Memorial Aviation Park 83
Doll's Head Trail 56
DuBois, W.E.B. 19
Eastern Continental Divide
Eastside Trail 13
Ebenezer Baptist Church 29, 40

Ellis Hotel 84
Emory University 73
Fernback Museum of Natural History 50
Foster House 85
Fourth Ward Park 70, 83
Fountain of the Rings 35
Georgia Aquarium 80, 81
Georgia Film Academy 63
Georgia Institute of Technology 72
Georgia State University 73
Gone With the Wind 21
Great Atlanta Fire 20
Gravel, Ryan 12
Gwinnett Stripers 67
Hartsfield-Jackson International Airport 25
Hartsfield, William 22
High Museum of Art 24, 48
Jackson, Maynard 23
King, Coretta Scott 28, 29
King Jr., Dr. Martin Luther 22, 27, 28, 29, 30
Krog Street Tunnel 47

94 Atlanta